About this Book

Imagine finding a pharaoh's tomb lost for three thousand years and still full of treasure! This is what happened to an Englishman called Howard Carter over fifty years ago when he was exploring in Egypt's Valley of the Kings. Since then, the splendid jewels, ornaments and furniture from the tomb of Tutankhamun have been shown in museums around the world.

Tutankhamun's Egypt tells the exciting story of Carter's discovery. It also shows us how people lived in those far-off days. We can see the young Pharaoh and his royal family; scribes and viziers; fierce archers and charioteers in Tutankhamun's army; and farmers peacefully tending their vines and herds. We can read about the temples, tombs and pyramids, and how and why the dead were mummified and buried with treasure.

Does all this seem very different from our own lives? Well, in their spare time Ancient Egyptians liked playing ball, board games and many of the activities we still enjoy today. And the girls wore make-up then, too!

Some of the words printed in *italics* may be new to you. You can look them up in the word list on page 92.

AN EYEWITNESS BOOK

Tutankhamun's Egypt

PENELOPE DAVIES & PHILIPPA STEWART

St. Martin's Press / New York

Wayland Publishers Limited / Hove, England

Frontispiece: Tutankhamun's coffin

SBN 85340 425 9
First published in the UK in 1978
by Wayland (Publishers) Ltd, 49 Lansdowne Place,
Hove, East Sussex BN3 1HF, England

St Martin's Press, Inc. 175 Fifth Ave.,
New York, N.Y. 10010
Library of Congress Catalog Card Number 77–92805
First published in the United States of
America in 1978

ISBN 0-312-82370-3 (paper edition)
ISBN 0-312-82369-X (cloth edition)

Text set in 14 pt Photon Univers, printed by photolithography, and
bound in Great Britain at The Pitman Press, Bath

Contents

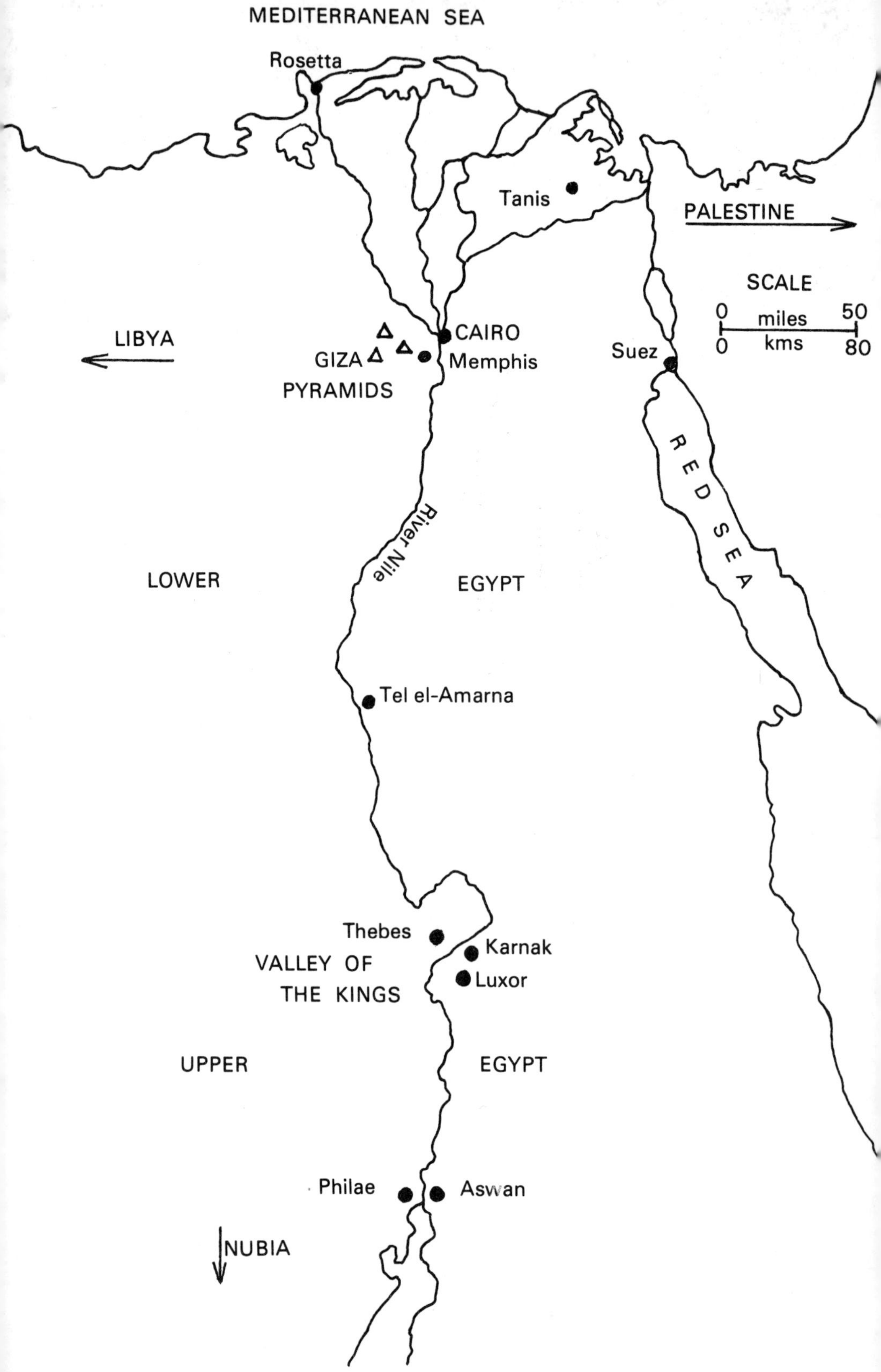

MEDITERRANEAN SEA

Rosetta

Tanis

PALESTINE →

← LIBYA

SCALE

0 miles 50
0 kms 80

△
GIZA △ △ ● CAIRO
PYRAMIDS ● Memphis

Suez

River Nile

R E D   S E A

LOWER

EGYPT

● Tel el-Amarna

Thebes ●
Karnak ●
VALLEY OF
THE KINGS
● Luxor

UPPER

EGYPT

Philae ● ● Aswan

↓ NUBIA

1. Tutankhamun's Kingdom

The boy pharaoh Tutankhamun came to the throne of Egypt around the year 1361 BC, when he was nine years old. (After all these years *archaeologists* are not absolutely certain of the date.) He ruled for nine years.

The splendid civilization of Ancient Egypt lasted for over three thousand years altogether. As the pictures in this book show, the Egyptians were great artists and craftsmen. Egypt was ruled by pharaohs. They were the equivalent of our kings and emperors. Most of the period was peaceful. The great River Nile running the length of the country flooded its banks each year. When the waters retreated in the summer heat, they left behind a *silt* that made the earth rich and fertile. The Egyptians called the Nile valley "the Black Land". Here they grew corn. In good years, they stored grain in granaries in case the next harvest was bad. They also sold some grain to other countries in exchange for goods they could not produce themselves. To either side of the river valley was a hostile world of mountains and deserts which the Egyptians called "the Red Land".

Because Egypt was so rich, other states sometimes attacked the country. But the Egyptians were not very often tempted to invade nearby countries. Ancient Egypt and its civilization survived for another thousand years after Tutankhamun. But by the time Christ was born, it had become just another province of the Roman Empire.

A UNITED COUNTRY Tutankhamun's kingdom
had not always been so large. Originally it was two
countries: Upper Egypt in the south and Lower
Egypt to the north. This ceremonial palette shows
Narmer, the first pharaoh of the united country. At
the bottom are the bodies of two of his enemies,
and he is killing a third. Behind him stands his
sandal-bearer. Notice that Narmer is much larger
than the others. This meant the pharaoh was more
important than anyone else.

RULED BY A GOD The union of the two
kingdoms was strengthened under the pharaohs
Cheops, Chephren and Mycerinus. The picture
shows Mycerinus and his wife. These rulers were
regarded as gods by their people. They ruled direct-

ly and personally from the capital city, Memphis. By the time Tutankhamun came to the throne, a thousand years later, a great *bureaucracy* had developed. Then the pharaoh took a less personal role.

9

TOMBS FIT FOR GODS   The Ancient Egyptians believed in life after death. They also regarded their pharaoh as a god. So a dead god-king needed a suitably grand tomb. This is the *pyramid,* or tomb, of Chephren, built around 2500 BC at Giza. It is 144 m (481 ft) high and has sides 235 m (786 ft) long. Over two million blocks of limestone, some weighing more than fifteen tonnes, were needed for it. (The pyramid of his father, Cheops, is even bigger!) Of course a structure this size took years to build. Most pharaohs started building their tomb

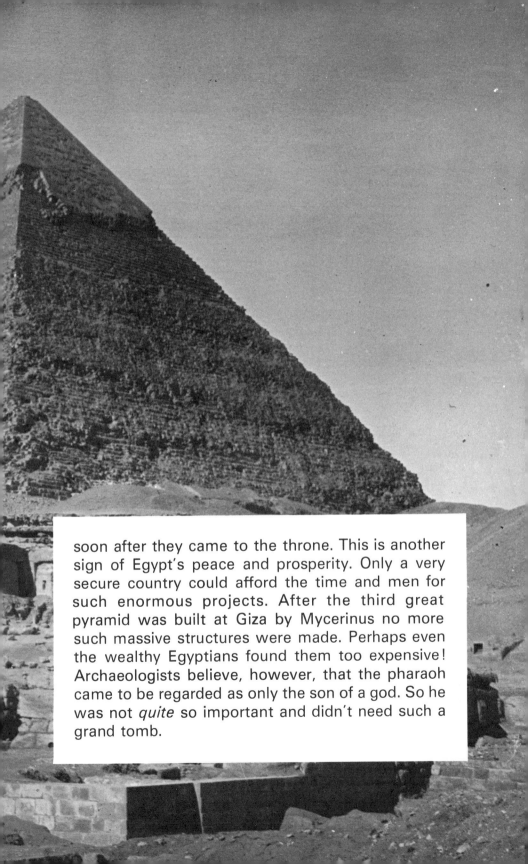

soon after they came to the throne. This is another sign of Egypt's peace and prosperity. Only a very secure country could afford the time and men for such enormous projects. After the third great pyramid was built at Giza by Mycerinus no more such massive structures were made. Perhaps even the wealthy Egyptians found them too expensive! Archaeologists believe, however, that the pharaoh came to be regarded as only the son of a god. So he was not *quite* so important and didn't need such a grand tomb.

INVASION! Around 1700 BC the settled life of Egypt was disrupted. To the north-east the great *Babylonian Empire* was breaking up. *Hittites* and *Hurrians* moved south and west into Syria, and the people already there were pushed into Egypt. They were called *Hyksôs*, or "Peoples of the Uplands". The man in the picture is one of them. They introduced horses and bronze to Egypt—an improvement on the copper Egyptian craftsmen had been using.

A REUNITED COUNTRY For over one hundred years foreigners ruled Egypt: the Hyksôs in the north and the *Nubians* in the south. They were finally driven out by the pharaoh Ahmose around 1570 BC. Upper and Lower Egypt again became one kingdom. This carving of Sethos I and two goddesses represents the reunion. The goddess on the right wears the tall crown of Upper Egypt, the southern kingdom. The other wears the crown of Lower Egypt. The pharaoh's crown, a combination of both, shows that with divine help he rules a united country.

14

2. The Government

When Tutankhamun became pharaoh around 1361 BC, Egypt was no longer ruled directly and personally by the king. Officials dealt with the everyday problems of running the kingdom. This was just as well when the pharaoh was weak or, like Tutankhamun, a child. At least the officials made sure the country did not grind to a halt. But without a strong pharaoh, intrigues and rivalries quickly developed. These could weaken the power of the government and the pharaoh.

The most important officials were the two *viziers,* or chief ministers. They were appointed by the pharaoh, one for Upper and one for Lower Egypt. They were responsible for everything in their part of the country. If they did the job badly, the pharaoh sacked them.

The country was divided into *nomes,* run by officials known as nomarchs. Under them were the mayors of the towns and the other local officials. Every detail of the work of all these men was recorded by *scribes.*

The Egyptians themselves had by now become conquerors. Syria, Palestine and Nubia were under their control. Taxes from these territories brought even more wealth to Egypt. To keep these regions loyal, they were governed by Egyptian *viceroys.*

This wall painting from inside a tomb shows Tutankhamun on his throne receiving *homage* from an important official. Notice the lines of pleating on the clothes the two men are wearing. In his left hand Tutankhamun holds his two sceptres, the crook of Upper Egypt and the flail of Lower Egypt. They stand for the unity of his kingdom.

A POWERFUL QUEEN   Scholars argue about who Tutankhamun's parents were. Some believe that Amenophis III and his wife, Queen Tiye, were his parents. Others think they were his grandparents. But we do know that Tiye was still very powerful during the reigns of Akhenaten and Tutankhamun. As you can see from this portrait head, she was not Egyptian. She probably came from Nubia. This shows just how clever she was. It was most unusual for a foreigner to achieve a powerful position in Egypt.

16

REWARDS FOR GOOD SERVICE The pharaoh appointed all his high officials. If they served him well the rewards could be great. Here, Akhenaten (the pharaoh before Tutankhamun) and his wife, Nefertiti, reward the official Ay by giving him gold necklaces. Ay was obviously a very clever man. He started as Master of Akhenaten's horses, virtually ran the country during Tutankhamun's reign, and finally made himself pharaoh when Tutankhamun died.

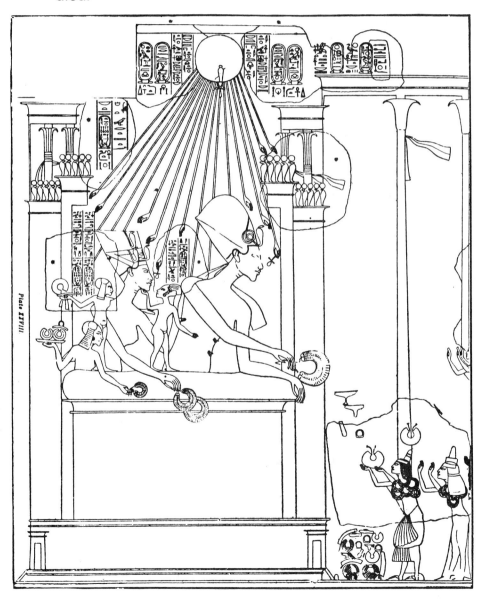

Plate LXVIII

TRANSPORT Pharaohs and officials had to travel around the country to carry out their work. The easiest way was by boat. Indeed, before horses were introduced into Egypt, it was almost the only way of moving about. Ferry boats like this one were rowed. But the larger, grander boats used by officials had masts and square sails as well.

A GOOD CIVIL SERVANT Good administrators were essential in a country as large as Egypt. One civil servant even listed his duties in his tomb! Another government official boasted that he "appointed the overseers on every estate throughout the province and charged them with the upkeep of three thousand head of cattle. When census time came round my efforts were praised by the Great House [the pharaoh]. No shortage was ever recorded in my delivery of the taxes." Perhaps the official shown opposite with his wife was as efficient!

THE SCRIBE A very important member of the Egyptian administration was the scribe. He made written records of everything that happened in the kingdom, to ensure that government ran smoothly. Scribes travelled throughout the land to write down the amount of crops in a nome, the number of new calves on a farm, and how many jars of wine had been pressed. Of course he recorded all the events like births, deaths, battles and treaties too. It is because many of these records still exist that we know so much about the Ancient Egyptians.

WRITING MATERIALS Scribes made their records on *papyrus,* an early form of paper made from the reeds that grew thickly along the Nile's banks. They wrote in red or black ink with reed pens. The *hieroglyphic* writing that we know from Egyptian carving was difficult to write quickly, so a shorthand form was developed. This is called *hieratic* writing. You can see from these pen cases that some scribes liked doodling!

A LOYAL VICEROY   Huy was undoubtedly Tutankhamun's best provincial ruler. He was appointed viceroy of Nubia soon after Tutankhamun became pharaoh and ruled the province wisely and well. He was given names like "fan-bearer on the king's right", "Divine Father", "intendant of Amun's cattle in the land of Kush". These titles were a sign of the pharaoh's special approval. Here he receives *tribute*—gold, slaves and cattle—from the Nubians on behalf of Tutankhamun. Notice the cone of perfume on his head.

3. Religion

The religion of Ancient Egypt was highly complicated. Each area once had its own gods. When the country was united, the people worshipped the pharaoh, too. According to the priests, the pharaoh represented Amun (or Amon-Re), the supreme being. Later the pharaoh's position changed and the priests became very powerful. This was partly because they were so rich. People made gifts to the temples of their chosen gods. But as the temples paid no taxes, the priests who looked after them enjoyed all this wealth.

Many Egyptian gods represented things common in the lives of the people. Jackals and ibises were both numerous. The god Anubis had the head of a jackal and Thoth, god of truth, had the head of the long-beaked ibis.

Of all the gods and goddesses, three of the most important were Horus, Isis and Osiris. You can see them in the picture opposite. Carvings often show Horus, the falcon-headed god, hovering just behind the pharaoh to give him divine protection. He was also painted on mummy cases, with his wings protectively outspread to help the dead person through the Underworld.

Respect for the dead and belief in a life after death played a very important part in Egyptian religion. The Egyptians thought that the dead faced a difficult journey through the twelve regions of the Underworld to the Celestial Fields. But they do not seem to have feared death—perhaps because things decay very slowly in the hot dry climate. In fact, archaeologists have found bodies older than any pharaoh which still look quite lifelike.

CREATING MAN   The gods were believed to be very interested in the lives of men, particularly pharaohs. Chnum, the ram-headed god, carefully models the image of a man on his potter's wheel. Behind him stands Thoth, the ibis-headed god, recording the number of years the man will live by notching them on a palm branch.

THE WEIGHING OF SOULS   Many Egyptians had a *Book of the Dead* buried with them, believing that its magical text would help their souls to the Celestial Fields. This picture comes from the *Book of the Dead* buried with the nobleman Ani and his wife. The jackal-headed god Anubis is weighing their souls against the Feather of Truth, to see if they are worthy to pass, while Thoth, god of truth, records the result. Behind him is the Devourer, a crocodile-headed monster who devours any souls who fail the test.

ISIS AND OSIRIS   Perhaps the most interesting of the gods and goddesses of Egypt were the sister and brother, Isis and Osiris. Egyptian legend tells how Osiris was killed by his jealous brother Seth, who chopped Osiris's body into a thousand pieces

and scattered them throughout the land. Devoted Isis traced each bit of her brother's mutilated body and buried it. Egyptians believed that Osiris then came to life again, and that it was his divine influence that made the crops in their fields grow tall.

HATHOR AND HOREMHEB   Cows were important in the Egyptian economy and the cow goddess, Hathor, was particularly popular. This statue shows her giving milk to Horemheb. He was a clever general who came to the throne a few years after Tutankhamun's death. He probably had this statue made for political reasons, to show the people that he had the support of the gods even though he was not of royal blood.

PRIESTS Priests were powerful and important members of Egyptian society. The many temples built to the different gods throughout the country were looked after by large numbers of priests. This little statue shows the priest Katep and his wife Hetepheres. The short kilt he is wearing shows that this statue is very old—over four thousand years—because later on full-length robes became fashionable.

A NEW RELIGION Some people felt the priests were becoming far too powerful. Akhenaten, the pharaoh before Tutankhamun, certainly thought so. He tried to break their power by starting a new type of religion. This had only one god, instead of the large numbers the Egyptians usually worshipped. This god, Aten, was represented as a sun disc with rays ending in hands, to show the life he gave to his people. Akhenaten built a new capital city, Tel el-Amarna, dedicated to the god. But the experiment was not successful, and when Akhenaten died the worship of Aten ceased.

MUMMIES   Preserving a person's body was an important part of Egyptian respect for the dead. To do this, a process called *mummification* developed. The dead person's insides, the parts that would rot, were removed and stored in airtight jars. Then linen, sawdust and spices were packed tightly into the body, padding it out to give a lifelike appearance. Next the body was swathed in bandages soaked in gum, which made them tacky and airtight. After many religious ceremonies, the mummy was adorned with a richly-jewelled mask and other decorations before being put in a painted coffin.

A DIFFICULT TASK When the archaeologist Howard Carter discovered the tomb of
Tutankhamun, one of his most difficult tasks was
dealing with the dead king's mummy. This was
enclosed inside three coffins so close-fitting that it
was hardly possible to put a finger between them.
Here Carter works on the mummy itself, in the third
and innermost coffin. He gently chips away at the
sacred oils and perfumes that were poured over the
mummy. Through the centuries, thcy have become
almost as hard as concrete.

33

4. Life in Tutankhamun's Egypt

In Ancient Egypt, even if a rich person could not read or write he could employ someone to write about him or paint portraits of himself and his family. So it is the wealthy people who have left us a great deal of information about themselves. Their tombs, like those of the pharaohs, were decorated with scenes from their daily lives and filled with models of objects from their earthly homes. But only a pharaoh could afford as rich a throne as this one from Tutankhamun's tomb!

Most of the people, however, were peasants and farmers who left no record of their lives. For them life revolved, as it always had, around the yearly flooding of the Nile. The flood was, in fact, their life. Without it there would have been no crops and, in a few years, the Black Land would have become as arid as the surrounding Red Land. And without it the people of the valley would have become nomadic, wandering people like the desert tribes they despised.

The invasions of the Hyksôs and the heresies of Akhenaten really affected only the top people in society. As long as the ordinary people paid their taxes they were left alone. They went on in the same old ways, believing them best. And if the fields went on producing good crops, why change?

AN OFFICIAL BANQUET   Banquets were popular with the royal court and wealthy members of society. This tomb painting shows important guests sitting on richly carved and decorated chairs, and those of lesser importance on stools. Knives and forks were unknown, so everyone ate with their fingers. They washed them between courses in sweet-scented water brought round by serving girls. Fillet steak, even then, was thought the best cut of meat. Wild-fowl from the great Nile marshes was also popular. At the bottom of the picture is a rack of wine jars. You can also see musicians and dancing girls entertaining the guests. Often there were acrobats, too.

A FASHIONABLE GUEST   Most Egyptian women worked hard, helping in the fields and bringing up their children. For the noble ladies, the princesses, the daughters and the wives of the pharaohs, life was much easier and more luxurious. They could spend hours adorning themselves with cosmetics and different shades of face powder, or combing their hair with fine ivory combs. For special occasions, like a state banquet, they wore little cones on their heads, filled with expensive perfume. Then, having chosen what jewellery to wear from the selection brought by their maids, they were ready to enjoy themselves.

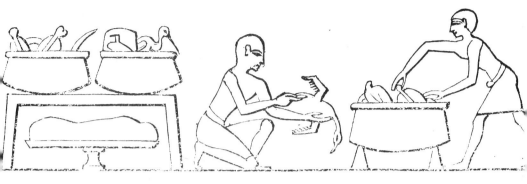

COOKING FOR A BANQUET Palace cooks worked for days before a grand state banquet. These cooks are preparing the meat and poultry. At the left of the top picture, different meats are waiting to be cooked. In the middle the cook prepares a goose for boiling in the large cauldron-like pot on the right. The cook in the picture below roasts a goose on a hand-held spit, fanning the fire to get an even heat, while on the right another does the carving.

BEDS Wealthy Egyptians liked their comfort, judging by the furniture found in their tombs. In Tutankhamun's there were eight beds, apart from all the other furniture! Of course the poor people could not afford such luxury. The bed in this picture once had "springs" of interwoven strips of leather.

TOYS The figure in the picture has her head on a hard, raised headrest. These uncomfortable "pillows" were used so that people did not spoil their elaborate wigs while they slept. Although this model was probably made for a tomb, it could have been a child's toy. Archaeologists have found many toys, especially dolls.

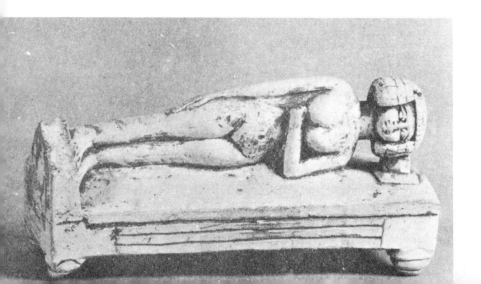

BOARD GAMES Board games were very popular among those Egyptians who had the leisure for such pastimes. The nobleman here plays on an oblong board divided into thirty squares. It may be a

kind of draughts, although this game has pieces of two different kinds. Notice how the man sits on a chair, while the woman has only a stool.

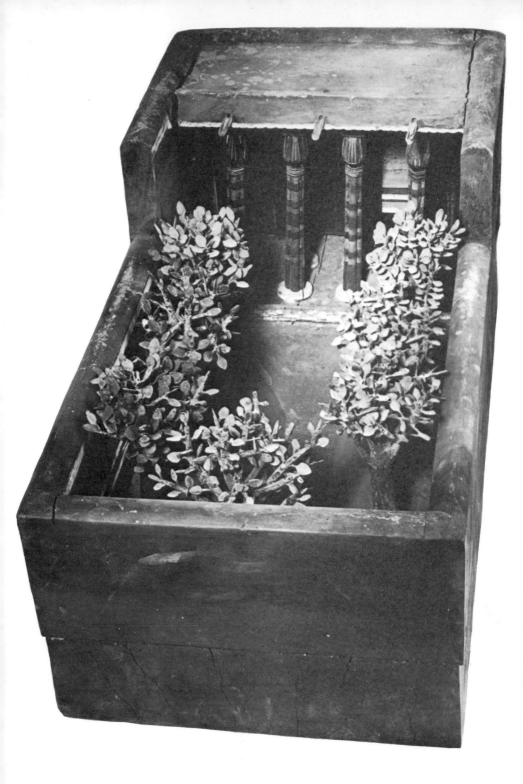

A GARDEN FOR ANOTHER WORLD　An important feature of most wealthy Egyptian homes was
the garden. It frequently had an ornamental pond.
Maket-Re, in whose tomb this model was found,
must have been very fond of his. Perhaps he hoped
to have one in the next world. See how beautifully
the columns are carved and painted.

A WORKMAN'S HOME　Of course, only the very
rich could afford lavish houses and gardens. Ordinary houses were fairly simple, usually built of
sun-dried mud bricks. This model house has two
storeys. The entrance in the middle is only for the
lower floor. The upper storey is reached by the outside staircase on the left, so perhaps two families
lived here.

HARPOONS AND BOOMERANGS Outdoor activities were popular, especially if they added to the family's larder. These two men have brought their families for a day out on the river. On the left, father and son use boomerangs to bring down the ducks and other birds flying up from the tall reeds. The other man fishes with a double-pointed harpoon.

HUNTING CAT This hunter's cat has caught a bird, too. It is another family outing. His wife is standing behind him, and his daughter is sitting at his feet.

HUNTING   After the Hyksôs brought the first
horses to Egypt, hunting swift gazelles and ostriches from horse-drawn chariots became popular
among the very rich. (Chariots and horses were too
expensive for anyone else.) Here the pharaoh
shoots ostriches with bow and arrow, his hound
running beside the chariot. Ostrich feather fans
were used a lot in the hot Egyptian summers. This
drawing comes from a fan.

FARMING   Most Egyptians were farmers. It was
agriculture that made the country rich. But even
with the great River Nile and its yearly flood, water
was still a problem for farmers. In the heat of
summer, fields could soon become dry and crops
die through lack of water. To prevent this, the Egyptians developed irrigation systems. These were
channels dug in the land and filled with water. One
invention which still makes the farmer's work much

easier is the *shaduf*. This is a bucket hanging from a weighted pole. The pole is raised to drop the bucket into the river. Then the pole is lowered, raising the heavy, water-filled bucket for the farmer to empty into one of the many irrigation channels surrounding his fields. Before the *shaduf* was invented, the farmer had to haul the heavy bucket up and down himself. The *shaduf* has been used since 1500 BC —which shows just what a good invention it is!

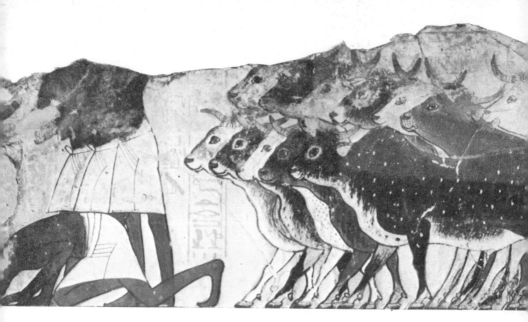

HERDS OF CATTLE The Egyptians liked meat—in one tomb there is a prayer asking the gods to be sure to give the dead man "beef and goose, bread and beer"! Herds of cattle, domesticated from the long-horned wild ones, were kept and fattened for beef. Large herds were a sign of wealth. Each year the number of cattle in a nobleman's herd was counted and recorded by scribes, as these tomb paintings show.

MILKING AND REAPING Cows were also kept for their milk. It was difficult to keep milk fresh in the hot climate, so the Egyptians probably drank a form of sour milk. It was also made into butter and cheese. Below the cows is a group of men cutting

corn. Wheat and barley were the grain crops. But they were not the large-grained varieties of today. In fact, *emmer*, the wheat of that time, would seem more like large grass seed to us!

PLOUGHING AND HARVEST-TIME Corn was harvested in two ways. Sometimes the whole stalk was cut and tied into bundles or sheaves (top left). At others, only the ear of grain at the top of the stalk was cut off and carried away in baskets (top middle). Notice the scribe with his pencase under his arm (top, 5th left); he records the harvest yield so that nothing is stolen. The corn was then loaded onto donkeys to be taken away for threshing. Donkeys had a reputation for stubbornness even then; the hieroglyphics above one picture of a loaded donkey read: "Ho ho, you slow-coach, gee up." The lower pictures show the Egyptians' ox-drawn ploughs. Fields were ploughed and the seed sown before the Nile's flood waters had dried. Otherwise the ground became too hard to plough or for the tiny seeds to grow in. A bow-shaped tool, a kind of hoe, was also used to prepare the ground.

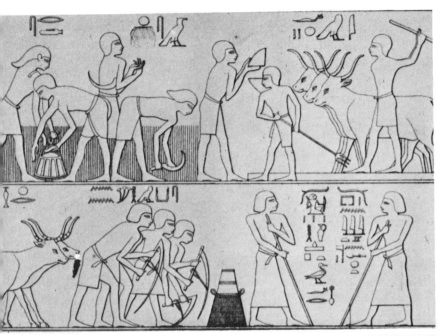

51

FRUIT AND VEGETABLES   We still use many vegetables which grew in Ancient Egypt—onions, beans, lentils, cucumbers and cos lettuce, for example. There was less choice of fruit—mainly figs, dates and grapes. Olives were not grown much before Tutankhamun's time, and even then they were rare. Wine was a popular drink with the wealthy. It was made by piling grapes into a press and treading on them until the juice ran out. These treaders hold onto ropes to keep their balance. Perhaps the dates also hanging from the top of the press were supposed to give them energy in their hard, hot task.

THRESHING THE CORN   After the corn had been harvested the grain had to be separated from the *chaff*. The corn was taken to the threshing floor, a special area of very hard ground. The corn was tipped onto it, while oxen, yoked across the horns, walked round and round, breaking the grain away from the light, useless chaff.

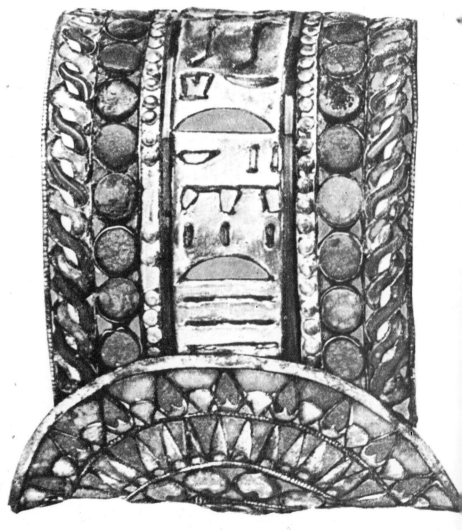

54

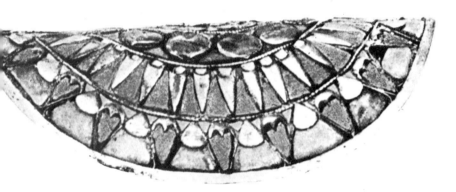

CRAFTSMEN Ancient Egypt was rich enough and peaceful enough for the people to spend time and money on luxuries. Even their useful objects were made in a lavish way. The amount of gold used by Egyptian craftsmen is amazing. Even these axles from a chariot in Tutankhamun's tomb are covered with gold and jewels. They also made fine jewellery and royal regalia. Many beautiful objects were so well-made that they have lasted almost perfectly. Most of the gold came from the Egyptian province of Nubia. The mines were run by the government and worked by gangs of slaves and criminals. The jewels used were mostly semi-precious—pearls, turquoise, jade, coral and lapis lazuli.

A CARPENTER'S SHOP   Egyptian carpenters had most of the tools still used today—saws, chisels, awls and hammers. But they used an *adze,* not a plane, to smooth surfaces. The man sawing planks in this carpenter's shop has lashed the piece of timber to a post to hold it steady. But the Egyptians had very little wood. Much of the wood that was used came from Lebanon. It was floated down to the Nile from Byblos, where the Egyptians started a colony around 2500 BC. The Old Testament of the Bible describes how the Jews also used cedarwood from Lebanon.

A CHEST FOR THE PHARAOH   This richly carved and gilded chest was found in the tomb of Amenophis III (*c* 1417–1379 BC). Because it was for a pharaoh, the craftsmen took great pride in showing their skills. But even in more humble articles the carpenters took care, neatly making joints still used—halved, mitred, concealed, and mortice-and-tenon. Plywood, too, isn't new. Carpenters were making it from six different layers of wood as early as 2800 BC!

58

STONE MASONS   The greatest and best-known work of all Egyptian craftsmen is that of the stone masons. Indeed, for many centuries it was the only aspect of the ancient civilization that anyone knew. It seems amazing, but even the *sphinx* had to be *excavated.* Here craftsmen carve two statues from blocks of stone and give a final polish to a sphinx. The workmen certainly needed scaffolding to reach the tops of these statues. And on one statue of Ramses II, his crown alone was 2 m (6½ ft) high!

ROPEMAKING AND CARPENTRY   Rope was essential in Egyptian transport. Without it, the giant statues would have been even more difficult to move. Beside the carpenter using the bow drill are several legs ready to be put on a piece of furniture.

BRICKMAKING AND BUILDING   Although the Egyptians sometimes fired bricks to harden them, they usually just left them outside for the sun to do it naturally. Here workmen collect and mould mud into bricks. The dried ones are being carried away for use. The man in the middle carefully makes sure that the new wall is straight.

BRONZE CASTING   Metal casting is dangerous work. These men use tongs to handle the container of molten bronze, carefully picking it up from the fire and pouring the metal into moulds (below). To get the fire really hot they use foot bellows (below left).

FINISHING TOUCHES   When metal items have been cast they need polishing and decorating (left). Then they are weighed, checked and recorded by the scribe (right). Only then could they be sold or delivered to the customer.

TRADE   Rich though Egypt was, the land did not provide everything the people wanted, so there was some trade with nearby states. These drawings record an Egyptian expedition to Punt (modern Somali Republic and Eritrea) for spices and incense trees. The traders thought the houses on stilts very odd!

BOATBUILDING The Nile was the highway of Ancient Egypt and boats were the main form of transport. They varied from tiny canoes made from bundles of papyrus to great tall-masted, square-sailed vessels, with many oarsmen, like this. One problem the boatbuilder faced was lack of good wood. Local trees, like fig and sycamore, gave narrow planks. This meant there were more joins where water could get in. But records—carved, painted and written—show that the problem was overcome and the river was alive with boats.

THE ARMY The Egyptians were not a particularly warlike race. They were satisfied with their own land, and there was little to tempt them in the surrounding countries. But sometimes they had to defend their borders from invaders. Tuthmosis III (c 1482–1450 BC) was one of the most warlike pharaohs. He built up the army and led a summer campaign each year for nearly twenty years in Palestine and Syria. These campaigns were so successful that even after his death Egypt kept control of these provinces for many years. These pictures show Jewish prisoners bringing the pharaoh tribute—horses, lions and precious objects. Defeated states had to pay heavy taxes, too.

EGYPTIAN INFANTRY Foot soldiers (infantry) were the main fighting force in the Egyptian army. Their chief weapons were bows and arrows, spears or boomerangs.

WAR CHARIOTS After horses were introduced to Egypt, chariots came into use in the army. Because of their expense they were probably used only by the pharaoh and a few great noblemen. Strangely, no one seems to have ridden a horse, so there was no cavalry.

CAPTURING A CITY Ramses II was another fearless and warlike pharaoh, but his campaigns were not always successful. He failed to drive the Hittites out of northern Syria, although all the accounts of this campaign make out that it was an Egyptian success! Here he is about to kill the general of a besieged Syrian fortress. The prisoners are led by the neck before him as he stands on the backs of two others.

70

5. Egypt after Tutankhamun

When Tutankhamun died at the age of eighteen, his kingdom was in disarray. He had come to the throne at nine years old, and never managed to control groups led by Queen Tiye and the Vizier Ay.

Ankhesenamun, Tutankhamun's young widow, desperately tried to stop Ay seizing power. She even offered to make an alliance with Egypt's enemy Shuppiluliumash, King of the Hittites. This was so amazing that the king did not believe it until it was too late. However, Ay's reign was short, for he was already an old man.

Horemheb took power next. He was a general, not of royal blood, and he set out to discredit Ay, Tutankhamun and Akhenaten. He ordered all mention of these pharaohs to be destroyed, whether on statues, in tomb paintings or state records, and claimed that the temples of Tutankhamun and Ay were really his.

In a way this was the beginning of the end of Egypt's greatness. Under Seti I and Ramses II Egypt again enjoyed a period of wealth, as this great temple built at Abu Simbel by Ramses shows. But stronger and newer states were growing up.

The Egyptians were so used to power that they were slow to change to new ideas. When the Hyksôs had attacked, the Egyptians' copper weapons were no match for the invaders' bronze. Now history was to repeat itself. The enemies who threatened the kingdom had weapons of iron, and great navies which swept down on the delta without warning. By 1000 BC the great kingdom had once more split into two parts. Foreign pharaohs ruled Lower Egypt from Tanis, and the priests of Amun ruled Upper Egypt from Thebes.

RAMSES II IN BATTLE Under Ramses II the Egyptians enjoyed the last of their military greatness when they defeated the Hittites. The army numbered twenty thousand men, including many men from countries controlled by Egypt. Some of the men were conscripts—people who did not volunteer but were forced by law to join the army.

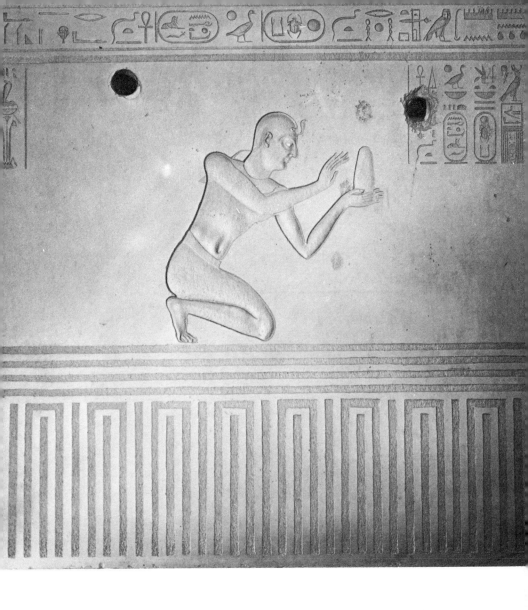

PSAMMETICOS, PRINCE OF SAIS Many of the foreign rulers of Egypt called themselves pharaoh, for it was still a respected title. After the Nubian and Libyan invaders came the *Assyrians.* But they were so unpopular that opposition to them grew under the the local princes of Sais. One, Psammeticos (655–610 BC), successfully overcame the Assyrians and became pharaoh himself.

MORE CONQUERORS   Now conquerors of Egypt seemed to come and go very quickly. The rulers from Sais were overthrown in 525 BC by the Persians under Cambyses, son of Cyrus the Great. Two hundred years later Alexander the Great defeated the Persians, and was himself made pharaoh. After Alexander's death in 323 BC, a general in his army took power, proclaiming himself Ptolemy I. You can see Ptolemy I in the picture.

THE DEATH OF A CIVILIZATION   The final rulers of Ancient Egypt were the Romans. It was no longer a great kingdom. Now it was just one province in a greater empire. Even the gods looked Roman. Compare this figure of Anubis with the one on page 27.

74

6. New Interest in Ancient Egypt

Today there is a great interest in archaeology and the past. It seems incredible to us that any civilization as splendid as that of Ancient Egypt could be forgotten. But it was. After the end of the Roman Empire travel became more difficult and much less safe. Few foreigners ever reached Egypt. Even if they had, there was remarkably little to see—sand, wind and time can bury even large statues most effectively. True, there were the pyramids and some of the tombs, but if a curious visitor asked about them he learned little. Everyone took them for granted. After all, no one could remember a time without them—they were built over two thousand years before the birth of Christ.

Over the centuries northern and western Europe became the most civilized areas. Settled and wealthy states developed there and people once more began to reach Egypt. When they saw the signs of its past they were amazed.

Surprisingly, Napoleon was one of the first people to take a scientific interest in the ancient monuments of Egypt. In 1798 he set out with his army to conquer the country. He also took scholars to note down what they found. Napoleon's rule of Egypt was short. He left the next year, and the French army followed in 1801. But he took back to France boatloads of souvenirs, Ancient Egyptian objects and the first scientific reports on the country.

THE CLUE TO EGYPT'S PAST This piece of black basalt rock is one of the biggest discoveries made by Napoleon's expedition in Egypt. Found near the fortress of Rosetta, and now called the Rosetta Stone, it is carved with a decree (order) glorifying Ptolemy V *c* 196 BC. The decree is given in three languages: Greek, *demotic* Egyptian and hieroglyphic Egyptian. This was to be very important in rediscovering the lost world of Ancient Egypt.

DECIPHERMENT AND DISCOVERY Napoleon realized the importance of the Rosetta Stone, and had copies sent to the leading scholars of Europe. The Englishman Dr Thomas Young and the Frenchman Jean François Champollion (below) were the first to *decipher* the hieroglyphics. They compared the Greek text on the stone, which they understood, with the two other long-forgotten Ancient Egyptian languages. The work was slow, and later scholars completed it. After that, the whole history of that great civilization, so carefully recorded by thousands of scribes over many centuries, could be revealed.

EARLY EXPLORERS OF THE PYRAMIDS

Napoleon was exceptional in his scholarly interest in Ancient Egypt. Most of the early visitors were interested but uninformed. Some of the accounts and drawings of their explorings are very odd! In this picture it looks as if the people are testing the coffins for size!

THE FIRST ARCHAEOLOGISTS　By late Victorian times archaeology was becoming a science. Flinders Petrie was one of the first to excavate scientifically, seeking information about the past, not just loot. This is a photograph of his expedition to the Valley of the Kings in 1894. Robbers had raided all the tombs except one. Many robberies were not even recent. There are records of the trials of tomb robbers during the time of the pharaohs.

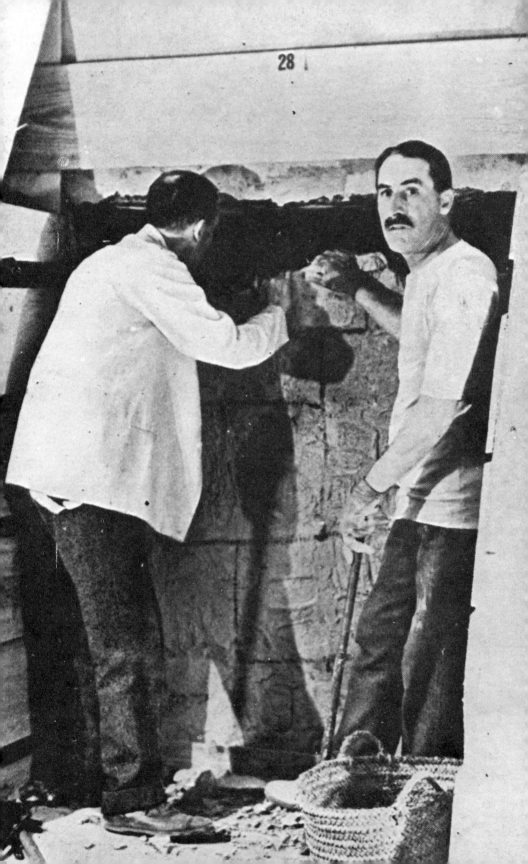

7. Discovering the Tomb

"It is my firm opinion that in the valley of Biban el-Maluk [the Valley of the Kings] there are no more unknown tombs," wrote the Italian explorer Belzoni in 1817.

Many archaeologists had visited and left the Valley of the Kings since Belzoni. Some had made finds, others had not. But by 1900 most were certain there was nothing more there.

In 1907, Lord Carnarvon, a wealthy Englishman, arrived in Egypt to recover from a serious illness. He became interested in Egyptian archaeology, and hired a young man, Howard Carter, to help him excavate in the Valley. Because of the upheavals of World War One, they could not start serious work until 1917.

That season produced nothing important. Nor did 1918. 1919, 1920 and 1921 were also unsuccessful. In the summer of 1922 Lord Carnarvon thought of ending the work. Carter begged to be allowed one more season. Work began again on 1st November, 1922. Two days later "an unusual silence" from the workmen alerted Carter. They had found a step, the first of sixteen leading down into the hillside. At the bottom was a doorway. Immediately Carter telegraphed Lord Carnarvon: "At last ... made wonderful discovery in Valley ... ."

Carnarvon travelled straightaway to Egypt. On 26th November the decisive moment came. Carter removed some stones from the doorway, held up a candle and looked through.

"Can you see anything?" asked Lord Carnarvon.

"YES", SAID CARTER, "WONDERFUL THINGS."

HANDLE WITH CARE Now the difficult work really started. The "wonderful things" of the young pharaoh Tutankhamun were all jumbled up in the tomb. He had been buried very quickly. But everything, like this hippopotamus-headed bed, had to be carefully disentangled and removed.

RECORDING THE FINDS Then everything was recorded. No matter how small the object, it was measured, described, drawn and entered in Carter's card index. Here he labels Tutankhamun's funeral wreath. It was the last object taken from the tomb.

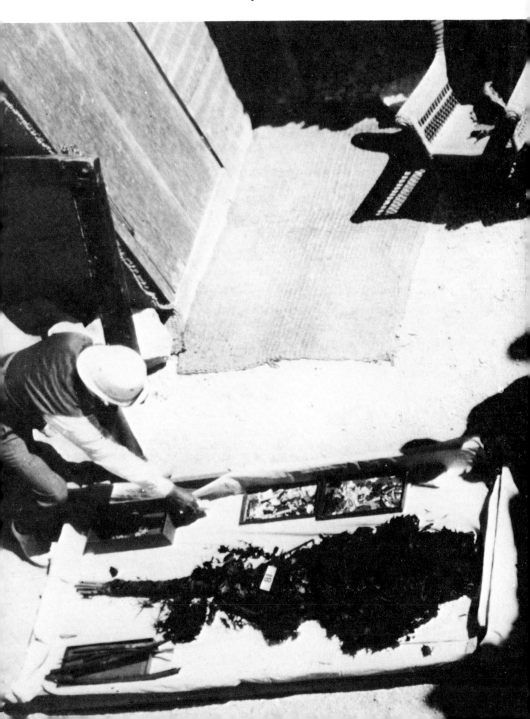

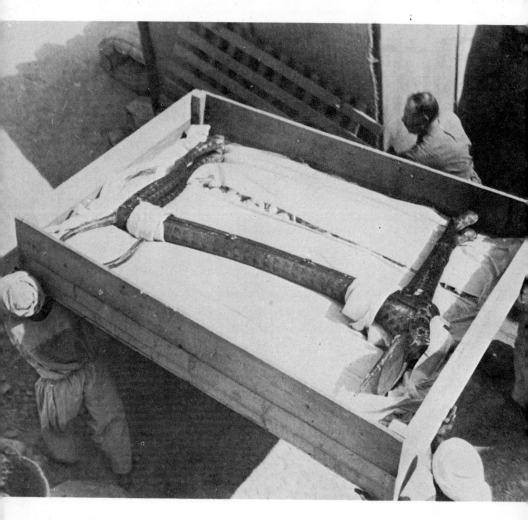

PACKING   Only after all this had been completed was an object packed and sent off to the Cairo Museum. Even this was difficult. The things were so precious and the path down to the railway so steep and rocky.

THE FINAL JOURNEY   The railway, specially built ᴛᴏʀ the purpose, carried the precious things to Luxor. Here they were loaded onto barges and taken to Cairo. So, once again, the pharaoh sailed on the great river of his kingdom.

A KING RESTORED   In 1972, to mark the fiftieth anniversary of Carter's discovery, some of the finest things from Tutankhamun's tomb were exhibited in London. This gold face mask from his mummy was particularly admired. More than $1\frac{1}{2}$ million people went to see the spectacular exhibition. Later it went to the United States of America for a three-year tour. Over 6,000 people a day visited it when it opened in the capital, Washington. So today, despite the efforts of Horemheb, more people know about Tutankhamun than when he ruled three thousand years ago.

Table of Dates

(After all these years, many of the dates in the earliest history of Egypt are not definitely known. The ones given here are the ones that scholars usually agree as being correct, but don't be surprised if you find a slightly different date in another book.)

New Words

Adze	Carpenter's tool used to cut or shape wood
Archaeologist	A person who seeks scientific facts about man's ancient past
Assyrians	Inhabitants of the ancient kingdom of Assyria which lay between the Tigris and Euphrates rivers
Babylonia	An ancient kingdom in what is now Iraq
Bureaucracy	Government by officials
Chaff	The dry, useless part surrounding the grain on an ear of corn
Decipher	To make out the meaning of something difficult, usually writing
Demotic	The popular, everyday form of a language or writing (opposite to *hieratic*)
Emmer	An early form of wheat
Excavate	To dig out. Excavating is one of the chief ways archaeologists obtain evidence about the past
Hieratic	The formal, official way of writing (opposite to *demotic*)
Hieroglyphs	Writing which uses symbols of objects to represent words and sounds. Sometimes called picture writing
Hittites	The people of an ancient empire in what is now Turkey and Syria

Homage	A public show of respect
Hurrians	A people originally from the area now called Armenia and divided between Russia, Turkey and Iran
Hyksôs	People from Syria and Palestine who invaded Egypt around 1775 BC
Mummification	The Ancient Egyptians' way of preserving a dead person's body
Nomes	The administrative areas into which Egypt was divided (like our counties)
Nubia	The region to the south of Egypt, extending from modern Khartoum to Aswan
Papyrus	A type of paper made from marsh and river reeds. The plural is papyri
Pyramid	Giant stone monument with a square base and sides which slope upwards to meet in a point. Generally built as a tomb for a pharaoh
Sarcophagus	A stone coffin
Scribe	Ancient Egyptian official employed to keep written records of events
Silt	Very fine sediment (soil) deposited by water, usually very rich and fertile
Sphinx	Ancient Egyptian mythical creature with a lion's body and the head of a man or an animal
Tribute	Money or gifts given by one state to another more powerful one, to show the submission of

	the weaker state
Viceroy	Someone appointed by the king to rule one of his provinces on his (the king's) behalf behalf
Vizier	High official. In Ancient Egypt one of the two chief ministers

More Books

Egypt by Anne Millard (Young Archaeologist series, Hart Davis, 1971). An insight into the work of archaeologists in Egypt. It describes individual finds and what they tell us.

Land of the Pharaohs by Leonard Cottrell (Brockhampton Press, 1962). Begins with the discovery of Tutankhamun's tomb, then goes back in time, describing through the eyes of a young nobleman what life was like in Ancient Egypt.

The First Book of Egypt by C A Robinson (Watts, 1965). Recreates the life of the Ancient Egyptians.

The Two Reigns of Tutankhamun by William Wise (Hamish Hamilton, 1966). Tells the story of Tutankhamun's life and the search for his tomb in the Valley of the Kings.

They Lived Like This in Ancient Egypt by Marie Neurath and John Ellis (Macdonald, 1964). Pictures and details of everyday life in Egypt about three thousand years ago.

(These last two books may be out of print, but try the library!)

Index

Picture Credits

The author and publishers wish to thank the following for giving permission to reproduce copyright illustrations on the pages mentioned: Radio Times Hulton Picture Library, 8, 10–11, 12, 14, 16, 20, 21, 26–27, 28, 30, 34, 41, 42, 46–47, 48, 49, 52–53, 57, 63, 66–67, 67 *top*, 72, 76, 78, 80, 81, 86, 87, 88, 89, 90; The Mansell Collection, 9, 13, 17, 18, 19, 22–23, 24, 27 *top*, 29, 31, 33, 36–37, 38, 39, 40, 43, 50–51, 52 *top*, 54, 56, 58–59, 62, 64–65, 68–69, 73, 74, 75, 82; The Trustees of the British Museum, 32, 45 *bottom*, 79; and Michael Paysden for the map on page 6.